Last Words Of The Dying

Douglas E. Casimiri

Other Books by the Author

Christians Remember Your Past Lives-Learn How

Live Your Life in AWE!

Undercover Uber

Whispers of Love

Past Lives A To Z

Whispered Last Words

2018 Douglas E. Casimiri. All rights reserved.

No part of this book may be reproduced, stored in a retrieval system, or transmitted by any means without the written permission of the author.

Published by Douglas Casimiri

ISBN-13: 978-1721731893

ISBN-10: 172173189X

Email: doug@positivepastlife.com

Web: positivepastlife.com

Last Words of the Dying

Introduction

The idea for this book came to me with the passing of David Cassidy. David's final words were "**So Much Wasted Time**". In my opinion, there has never been a truer statement. Just think about how much time we all have been wasting throughout our lifetimes.

Just to show you how short our lives are, if we took the total time earth has been in existence and we condense that time into one year. Man has been here for one second of that one year. Let that thought resonate for a moment.

David and I met in Las Vegas, at that time David was the headliner at MGM Hotel. David lived next door to friends of mine and we spent some time together and became quite close.

So, the final words of David Cassidy have motivated me to think about others who have passed on and their final words. What messages they left behind for us to discover?

My background is that of a Past Life Regression Facilitator. What is that you ask?

In simple terms, I take people back in time to a lifetime they lived prior to their present lifetime. I have written books on the subject. It's because of my background in dealing with past lives, death and rebirth this question came to my mind. If the words at the time of death have any effect on our present lives?

I have spent a lot of time researching the dying words of Presidents, famous people, Saints, criminals and just everyday individuals. I believe that people tend to become the most honest when they are about to die. Some believe; of all the words we have spoken throughout our lifetimes, it is what we say on our death bed that makes the most sense.

Remember this, you don't want to go to your grave with regrets crying "I wish I would have". You want to arrive at death's door screaming **"WOW what a ride".** I hope you find these last words of the dying fascinating. Maybe you will find special message that will have a profound effect on the direction of your life.

Contents

Introduction	3
U.S. Presidents Last Words	6
Celebrities and Others	27
The Saints	73
Criminals	87
Last Word Stories	73
My Thoughts on Saying Goodbye	110
My Conclusion About Last Words of the Dying	113
About the Author	116

U.S. Presidents Last Words

George Washington

Born in Virginia on February 22, 1732 – died December 14, 1799 at his home in Mount Vernon. George Washington was 67 years old.

George Washington was an American statesman and soldier who served as the first President of the United States from 1789 to 1797. One of the founding fathers of the United States and served as Commander-in-chief of the Continental Army during the American Revolutionary war.

George Washington's last words: I am just going. Have me decently buried and do not let my body be put into the vault in less than three days after I am dead? I guess George might have been afraid they may bury him alive.

Cause of Death: Epiglottitis; inflammation to the flap at the base of the tongue that keeps food from going into the trachea.

John Adams

Born in Braintree Massachusetts, on October 30, 1735 – died July 4, 1826 in Quincy, Massachusetts. John was 91 years old.

An American stateman and founding father. Served as first vice-president and second president of the United states.

John Adams last words: It is a glorious Fourth of July. It is a great day. God bless it, God bless you all. He later mumbled Thomas Jefferson's name at the same moment Thomas Jefferson died. They died with hours of each other on the fiftieth anniversary of the signing of the declaration of independence

Cause of Death: Congestive heart failure.

Thomas Jefferson

Born in Shadwell, Virginia on April 13, 1743 – died July 4, 1826 in Charlottesville, Virginia. Thomas was 83 years old.

Thomas Jefferson was the principal author of the declaration of Independence and later served as the third President of the United States from 1801 to 1809.

Thomas Jefferson's last words: Is it the fourth? I resign my spirit to God, my daughter to my country.

I find it truly amazing that John Adams and Thomas Jefferson died within hours of each other on July 4, 1826. Fifty years to the day after the signing of the Declaration of Independence.

Cause of Death: Bacteremia, bacteria in the blood.

James Madison

Born in Port Conway, Virginia on March 5, 1750 – died June 28, 1836 at his home Montpelier located in Orange, Virginia. James Madison was 86 years old.

James Madison was one of the founding fathers and served as the fourth President of the United States from 1809 to 1817. He was hailed as the father of the constitution for his pivotal role in the drafting and promoting the United States and the Bill of Rights.

James Madison last words: Nothing more than a change of mind, my dear. I always talk better lying down.

Cause of Death: Heart failure

James Monroe

Born in Virginia on April 28, 1758 – died on July 4, 1831 in New York City. James was 73 years old.

James Monroe was one of the founding fathers and served as the fifth President of the Unites States from 1817 to 1825.

James Monroe last words: I regret that I should leave this world without again beholding him. (Referring to James Madison)

Again, I find the date of his death fascinating. Another founding father dies on July fourth.

Cause of Death: Natural causes

John Quincy Adams

Born in Braintree, Massachusetts on July 11, 1767 – died February 23, 1848 in Washington, DC. John was 80 years old.

John was the sixth President of the United States from 1825 to 1829. He was the son of John Adams and his wife Abigail. John Adams was the second President of the United States.

John Quincy Adams last words: This is the last of the earth. I am content. John actually had a stroke on the floor of the house of representatives and died in the speaker's room in the capital building.

Cause of Death: Natural causes.

Andrew Jackson

Born on March 15, 1767 in Waxhaw's which borderers North and South Carolina – died on June 8, 1845 in his home Hermitage which is about 10 miles from Nashville, Tennessee. Andrew Jackson was 78 years old.

Andrew served as the seventh President of the United States from 1829-1837. He sought to advance the rights of the common man against the corrupt aristocracy and to preserve the union.

Andrew Jackson's last words: I hope to meet you all in heaven. Be good children, all of you, and strive to be ready when change comes.

Cause of Death: Natural causes.

Martin Van Burren

Born in New York on December 5, 1782 – died July 24, 1862 in New York. Martin Van Burren was 79 years old.

Martin was the founder of the Democratic Party and served as the eighth President of the United States from 1837 to 1841.

Martin Van Burren's last words: There is but one reliance….

Cause of Death: Heart failure

William Henry Harrison

Born in Virginia on February 9, 1773 – died on April 4, 1841 in Washington DC. William Henry Harrison was 78 years old.

William was an American Military officer and the ninth Present of the United States. He died of pneumonia just 31 days into his term. Thereby serving the shortest tenue in the United States as President.

William Henry Harrison last words: Sir, I wish you to understand the true principals of government. I wish them to be carried out. I ask nothing more.

Cause of Death: Sepsis

John Tyler

Born in Virginia on March 29, 1790 – died on January 18, 1862 in Richmond, Virginia. John Tyler was 72 years old.

John Tyler was the tenth President of the United States serving from 1841 to 1845.

John Tyler's last words: Doctor I am going. I hope not, said the doctor. Perhaps its best, said John Tyler.

Cause of Death: Stroke

James Polk

Born in Pineville, North Carolina on November 2, 1795 – died on June 15, 1849 in Nashville. Tennessee. James Polk was 54 years old.

James served as the 11th President of United States from 1845 to 1849.

James Polk last words: I love you Sarah for all eternity. I love you. (spoken to his wife).

Cause of Death: Cholera

Zachary Taylor

Born in Barboursville, Virginia on November 24, 1784 – died on July 9, 1850 in Washington DC. Zachary Taylor was 65 years old.

Zachary was the 12th president of the United States from 1849 to 1850. National hero as a result of his victories in the Mexican- American war.

Zachary Taylor last words: I am about to die. I expect the summons very soon. I regret nothing. I have tried to discharge all my duties faithfully. But I am sorry to leave my friends.

Cause of Death: Gastroenteritis, inflammation of the gastrointestinal tract.

Millard Fillmore

Born in Summerhill, New York on January 7, 1800 – died on March 8, 1874 in Buffalo, New York. Millard Fillmore was 74 years old.

Millard was the 13th president of the United States from 1850 to 1853.

Millard Fillmore last words: Accepting a spoonful of soup from his doctor. Millard Stated: the nourishment is palatable.

Cause of Death: Stroke

James Buchanan

Born in Lancaster, Pa on April 23, 1791 – died on June 1, 1868 in Lancaster, Pa. James Buchanan was 77 years old.

James Buchanan was the 15th President of the Unites States serving from 1857 to 1861. Historians fault him for his failure to prevent the secession of the southern states, which led to the civil war.

James Buchanan last words: Whatever the result may be. I shall carry to my grave the consciousness that at least I meant well for my country. Oh Lord God Almighty, as thou wilt.

Cause of Death: Natural causes

Abraham Lincoln

Born in Kentucky on February 12, 1809 – died on April 15, 1865 in Washington DC. Abraham Lincoln was assassinated at the age of 54.

Abraham Lincoln was the 16th President of the United States, served from 1861 until his assassination on April 15, 1865. Lincoln led the United States through the civil war.

Abraham Lincoln last words: Lincoln's final utterance was laughter during the performance of the play Our American Cousin.

Cause of Death: Assassination.

Andrew Johnson

Born in Raleigh, North Carolina on December 29, 1808 – died on July 31, 1875 in Elizabethton, Tennessee. Andrew Johnson was 66 years old.

Andrew Johnson was the 17th President of the United States and served from 1865 to 1869.

Andrew Johnson last words: After falling out of his chair, he said to his daughter. My right side is paralyzed. I need no Doctor. I can overcome my troubles.

Cause of Death: Stroke

Ulysses Grant

Born in Point Pleasant, Ohio on April 27, 1822 – died on July 23, 1885 in Wilton, New York. Ulysses Grant was 63 years old.

Ulysses Grant was a General during the Civil war and served as the 18th President of the United States from 1869 to 1877.

Ulysses Grant last words: Grant was suffering from throat cancer and couldn't speak much but did manage to ask for water just before he died. He did write; There was never one more willing to go than I am.

Cause of Death: Throat cancer.

Rutherford Hayes

Born in Fremont, Ohio on October 4, 1822 – died on January 17, 1893 in Fremont Ohio. Rutherford Hayes was 70 years old.

Rutherford Hayes was the 19th President of the United States served from 1877 to 1881.

Rutherford Hayes last words: I know I am going where my beloved Lucy is. Lucy was his wife who died four years earlier.

Cause of Death: Natural causes

James Garfield

Born in Cleveland, Ohio on November 19, 1831 – died on September 19, 1881 in New Jersey. James Garfield was 50 years old.

James Garfield was the 20th President of the United States served in office in 1881 until his assassination.

James Garfield last words: Said to his chief of staff, David Swaim. Oh, Swaim there is a pain here. Swaim can't you stop this? Oh, oh Swaim. Garfield who had been shot by an assassin month before, awoke clutching his heart and spoke these final words.

Cause of Death: Sepsis

Grover Cleveland

Born in New Jersey on March 18, 1837 – died on June 24, 1908 in Princeton, New Jersey. Grover Cleveland was 70 years old.

Grover Cleveland was the 22nd and the 24th President of the United States.

Grover Cleveland last words: I have tried so hard to do the right thing.

Cause of Death: Myocardial infarction

Benjamin Harrison

Born in Spain on August 20, 1833 – died on March 13, 1901 in Indianapolis, Indiana. Benjamin Harrison was 67 years old.

Benjamin Harrison was the 23rd President of the United States and served from 1889 to 1893.

Benjamin Harrison last words: Are the Doctors here? Doctor…. my lungs. Harrison died of pneumonia.

Cause of Death: Pneumonia

William McKinley

Born in Niles, Ohio on January 29, 1843 – died on September 14, 1901 in Buffalo, New York. William McKinley was 57 years old.

William McKinley was the 25th President of the United States serving from March 4, 1897 until his assassination in September 1901.

William McKinley last words: Good-bye, all. We are all going. It's God's way. His will be done, not ours. Nearer my God, to thee. We are all going. We are all going.

Cause of Death: Ballistic trauma (gunshot wound)

Theodore Roosevelt

Born in New York on October 27, 1858 – died on January 6, 1919 in Oyster Bay, New York. Theodore Roosevelt was 59 years old.

Theodore Roosevelt was the 26th President of the United States and served from 1901 to 1909.

Theodore Roosevelt last words: Please put out the light. He was speaking to his valet right before he went to bed and never woke up.

Cause of Death: Natural causes

Woodrow Wilson

Born in Staunton, Virginia on December 28, 1856 – died on February 3, 1924. Woodrow Wilson was 68 years old.

Woodrow Wilson served as the 28th President of the United States from 1913 to 1921.

Woodrow Wilson last words: I am a broken piece of machinery. When the machine is broken, I am ready.

Cause of Death: Natural causes

Warren Harding

Born in Blooming Grove, Ohio on November 2, 1865 – died on August 2, 1923 in San Francisco. Warren Harding was 57 years old.

Warren Harding was the 29th President of the United States and served from March 4, 1921 until his death in 1923.

Warren Harding last words: That's good read some more. His wife was reading him flatting accounts of him from the newspaper.

Cause of Death: Heart failure

Calvin Coolidge

Born in Plymouth Notch, Vermont on July 4, 1872 – died on January 5, 1933 in Northampton, Massachusetts. Calvin Coolidge was 59 years old.

Calvin Coolidge was the 30th President of the United States and served from 1923 to 1929.

Calvin Coolidge last words: Good morning Robert, he said to a carpenter working on his home.

Cause of Death: Coronary thrombosis.

Herbert Hoover

Born in West Branch, Iowa on August 10, 1874 – died on October 20, 1964. Herbert Hoover was 90 years old.

Herbert Hoover was the 31st President of the United States and served from 1929 to 1933.

Herbert Hoover last words: When told that Admiral Strauss had come to pay him a visit, Hoover was already speaking in the past tense. Hoover said: Levi Strauss was one of my best friends.

Cause of Death: Colorectal cancer

Franklin Roosevelt

Born in Hyde Park, New York on January 30, 1882 - died on April 12, 1945 in Warm Springs, Georgia. Franklin Roosevelt was 63 years old.

Franklin Roosevelt was the 32nd President of the United States. He served from 1933 to his death in 1945.

Franklin Roosevelt last words: I have a terrific headache. He died of a cerebral hemorrhage.

Cause of Death: Stroke

Dwight Eisenhower

Born in Denison, Texas on October 14, 1890 – died on March 28, 1969. Dwight Eisenhower was 78 years old.

Dwight Eisenhower was the 34th President of the United States and served from 1953 to 1961.

Dwight Eisenhower last words: I have always loved my wife, my children my grandchildren and my country. I want to go. Take me.

Cause of Death: Heart failure

John Kennedy

Born in Brookline, Massachusetts on May 29, 1917 – died on November 22, 1963.

John Kennedy was the 35th President of the Unites States and served from 1961 until his assassination in 1963. He was 46 years old.

John Kennedy last words: My God I have been hit.

Cause of Death: Assassination

Lyndon Johnson

Born in Stonewall, Texas on August 27, 1908 – died on January 22, 1973 in Stonewall, Texas. Lyndon Johnson was 64 years old.

Lyndon Johnson was the 36th President of the United States and served from 1963 to 1969.

Lyndon Johnson last words: Send Mike immediately! To a secret service agent over the telephone which was stationed 100 yards away. Time the agents got there Johnson was dead.

Cause of Death: Myocardial infarction

Richard Nixon

Born in Yorba Linda, California on January 9, 1913 – died on April 22, 1994 in Manhattan, New York. Richard Nixon was 81 years old.

Richard Nixon was the 37th President of the United States and served from 1969 to 1974. Ended the V

Richard Nixon last words: Help! He called out to his housekeeper. A stroke then left him mute he died the next day.

Cause of Death: Stroke

Ronald Regan

Born in Tampico, Illinois on February 6, 1911 – died June 5, 2004. Ronald Regan was 93 years old.

Ronald Regan was the 40th President of the Unites States and served from 1981 to 1989 and considered one of the greatest of all the Presidents. He ended the cold war with the Soviet Union by a policy of trust but verify through strength. President Ronald Regan restored the pride in the U.S. Military and re-established worldwide respect for the United States.

Ronald Regan Last words: Patti Davis his daughter described his death. At the last moment he opened his eyes and looked straight at my mother. With eyes that haven't opened in days. The eyes were clear and blue and full of love that expression was the greatest gift he could have ever given me and my mother. If a death can be lovely, his was. Then my mother said to her husband I love you.

Cause of Death: Alzheimer's disease

Celebrities and Others

Elvis Presley

Born in Tupelo, Mississippi January 8, 1935 – died August 16, 1977 at his home, Graceland, Memphis, Tn. Elvis was 42 years old.

In the year 2000 as we moved into the 21 centuries, Time magazine announced the most important person of the 20th century (last 100 years). That was Elvis Presley.

Over I billion records sold. Most hit singles 151 between 1956-1996.

Most records sold as per the Recording Industry Association of America certificates based on the number of albums and singles sold through retail, 235 total certificates, with 132 gold, 70 platina and 35 multi-platinum albums.

Ginger Alden, Elvis fiancé said Elvis told her he couldn't sleep, "he was going to the bathroom to read." That was Elvis Presley's last words and the rest as they say is history.

Elvis Presley's last words: I am going to the bathroom to read.

Cause of Death: Heart attack

Frank Sinatra

Born in Hoboken, New Jersey on December 12, 1915 - died May 14, 1982. Frank Sinatra was 82 years old.

Singer/actor who sold over 150 million records worldwide.

Frank Sinatra last words: "I'm losing it", I'm losing it". This is the first and last time when Frank wasn't in control.

Cause of Death: Myocardial infarction

Michael Jackson

Born in Gary, Indiana August 29, 1958 – died June 25, 2009 in Los Angeles, California. Michael Jackson was 50 years old.

Singer who sold over 750 million records worldwide.

Michaels last words were: "Let me have some milk", the phase he used when he wanted the white colored anesthetic Propofol drug that knocked him out. I guess with all the accusations against him I would want to be knocked out to.

Cause of Death: Drug overdose

Gustav Mahler

Born in Austria July 7, 1860 – died May 18, 1911. Gustav was 51 years old.

One of the leading conductor composers of his generation, died in bed, conducting an imaginary orchestra.

Gustav Mahler last words: was "Mozart". Doesn't it make you wonder if he saw Mozart as he was dying? I guess we will never know.

Cause of Death: Pneumonia

George Orwell (real name Eric Arthur Blair)

Born in India on June 25, 1903 – died January 21, 1950 in London, England. Eric Blair was 46 years old.

English Novelist and famous syfy writer, known for the dystopian "Nineteen Eighty-Four and Animal Farm,

George Orwell last words: "Don't let this nightmare situation happen. It depends on you". Here Eric was talking about the nightmare of nuclear war. So far so good George, we haven't destroyed ourselves yet.

Cause of Death: Accident

Bob Hope

Born in London, England on May 29, 1903 – died on July 27, 2003 in Los Angeles, CA. Bob Hope was 100 years old.

Bob Hope was an American actor, comedian, singer, dancer and author. Bob Hope entertained our troops around the world. Made numerous movies.

Bob Hope's last words: His wife Delores asked him where he wanted to be buried. He said surprise me.

Cause of Death: Pneumonia

Luciano Pavarotti

Born in Modena, Italy on october12, 1935 – died in Modena, Italy on September 6, 2007. Luciano Pavarotti was 71 years old.

Luciano Pavarotti was an Italian operatic tenor who crossed over into popular music, eventually becoming one of the most commercially successful tenors of all time.

Luciano Pavarotti last words: I believe that a life lived for music is an existence spent wonderfully, and this is what I have dedicated my life to.

Cause of Death: Pancreatic cancer

Nostradamus

Born in France on December 14, 1503 – died July 2, 1566 in Salon-de-Provence, France. Nostradamus was 62 years old.

He was a French Doctor. Reputed seer, who's published collection of prophecies have been studied throughout the centuries.

Nostradamus last words: "Tomorrow, at sunrise, I shall no longer be here." I guess Nostradamus was right, he predicted is own death and at sunrise he was no longer here, he was dead.

Cause of Death: Congestive heart failure

Joanie Chyna Laurer

Born in Rochester, NY on December 27, 1969 – died on April 20, 2016 in Redondo Beach, CA. Chyna was 46 years old.

Joanie Chyna Laurer was an America professional wrestler, glamour model, pornographic film actress and bodybuilder. She also appeared in Playboy Magazine and numerous television shows.

Chyna's last words: I just want y'all to have a beautiful, beautiful day today and I am sure be posting more things as the day goes on "cause" I will have all my friends here.

Cause of Death: Drug overdose

Edgar Allen Poe

Born in Boston, Ma. On January 19, 1809 – Died October 7, 1849 in Baltimore, MD. Edgar Allen Poe was 40 years old.

Edgar Allen Poe was an American author, poet, editor and literary critic, considered part of the American Romantic Movement. Best known for his tales of mystery and macabre, Poe was one of the earliest American practitioners of the short story.

Edgar Allen Poe last words: Lord help my poor soul.

Cause of Death: Remains a mystery, suicide, murder? He spent his last few days in fits of delirium and hallucinations. Some of it seemed associated with alcohol withdrawal.

Margaret Sanger

Born in Corning, New York September 14, 1879 – died September 6, 1966 in Tucson. Arizona. Margaret was 86 years old.

Margaret was an American birth control/abortion activist, that established organizations that evolved into Planned Parenthood. **Margaret Sanger last words were** "A party! Let's have a party." Do you think she was also thinking?" I hope everyone brings birth control".

Cause of Death: Atherosclerosis

Orson Wells

Born in Kenosha, WI on May 6, 1915 – died on October 10, 1985 in Hollywood, CA. Orson Wells was 69 years old.

Orson Wells was a stage actor before going on to radio, creating his unforgettable version of H.G. Wells War of the worlds. In film great works such as Citizen Kane and the Magnificent Ambersons.

Orson Wells last words: Talking into an answering machine; this is your friend. Don't forget to tell mw how your Mother is.

Cause of Death: Heart attack

Lou Costello

Born in Patterson, NJ on March 6, 1906 – died March 3, 1959 in Beverly Hills, CA. Lou Costello was 50 years old.

Lou Costello was an American actor of radio, stage, television and film. He is best remembered for the comedy double act of Abbott and Costello.

Lou Costello last words: That was the best ice-cream soda I ever tasted.

Cause of Death: Heart Attack

Selena

Born in Lake Jackson TX on April 16, 1971 – died on March 31, 1995 in Corpus Christi, TX. Selena was 24 years old.

Selena was considered the Queen of Tejano a type of Mexican music that incorporated other styles such as country. She was referred to as the Mexican Madonna for her sexy outfits and dance.

Selena's last words: She was mortally wounded and identified Saldiver her killer. Last words Yolanda room 158.

Cause of Death: Shot in the back. Murder

Marie Antoinette

Born an Archduchess of Austria in Austria on November 2, 1755 – died October 16, 1793 in France. Marie was 37 years old.

She was the last queen of France before the French revolution. On her way to beheaded by the guillotine, Marie Antoinette accidently stepped on her executioner's foot.

Marie Antoinette last words were "pardon me sir." Obviously, she still had style and grace on the way to be executed.

Cause of Death: Execution

B.B. King

Born in Itta Bena, MS. on September 16, 1925 – died on May 14, 2015 in Las Vegas, NV. B.B. King was 89 years old.

B. B. King was known as the King of Blues. He won his 15th Grammy Award in 2009. Great songs such as "The Thrill is Gone."

B.B. King's last words: The thrill is gone, but one way to get it back is to admit Pete Rose into the Hall of Fame.

Cause of Death: Vascular dementia

Stonewall Jackson

Born in Clarksburg, WV on January 21, 1824 – died on May 10, 1863 in guinea, VA. Stonewall Jackson was 39 years old.

Stonewall Jackson was a Confederate general during the American Civil War, and best-known Confederate commander after General Robert E. Lee.

Stonewall Jackson's last words: Let us cross over the river and sit in the shade of the trees.

Cause of Death: Firearm-Pneumonia

Tiny Tim

Tiny Tim born in New York City, NY on April 12, 1932 – died on November 30, 1996. Tiny Tim was 63 years old.

Tiny Tim is best remembered for playing his ukulele with songs like Tiptoe Through the Tulips, Livin in the Sunlight, Lovin in the Moonlight.

Tiny Tim's last words: And so, god bless us, everyone.

Cause of Death: Heart Attack

Thomas Edison

Born in Milan, Ohio on February 11, 1847 – Died on October 18, 1931 in West Orange, New Jersey. Thomas Edison was 84 years old.

Thomas Edison was an American inventor and businessman. He developed many devises that greatly influenced life around the world, including the phonograph, the motion picture camera, and a long-lasting practical electric light bulb.

Thomas Edison's last words: It is very beautiful over here.

Cause of Death: Diabetes mellitus

Paul Walker

Born in Glendale, CA on September 12, 1973 – died on November 30, 2013 in Santa Clarita, CA. Paul Walker was 39 years old.

Paul Walker was an American actor who became famous in movies such as Varsity Blues and The Fast and the Furious.

Paul Walkers last words: We will be right back in five minutes.

Cause of Death: Motor vehicle accident

Chief Sitting Bull

Born in South Dakota in 1831 – died December 15, 1890 in the Standing Rock Indian reservation. Chief Sitting Bull was 59 years old.

Chief Sitting Bull was a Hunkpapa Lakota holy man who led his people as tribal chief during the years of fighting with the US government. He was killed by Indian Agency during an attempt to arrest him.

Chief Sitting Bull last words: I am not going. Do with me what you like. I am not going. Come on! come on! Take action. Let's go. I guess he got what he asking for.

Cause of Death: Assassination

Marvin Gaye

Born in Washington, DC on April 2, 1939 – died on April 1, 1984 in Los Angeles, CA. Marvin Gaye was 45 years old.

Marvin Gaye was known as the prince of Soul. He was inducted into the The Rock and Roll Hall of fame in 1987. Marvin Gaye made a huge contribution to soul music.

Marvin Gaye's last words: Mother I am going to get my things and get out of this house. Father hates me and I am not coming back.

Cause of Death: Murder by his father

George Bernard Shaw

Born in Dublin, Ireland on July 26, 1856 – died November 2, 1950. George Bernard Shaw was 94 years old.

George Bernard Shaw was an Irish playwright and co-founder of the London School of Economics. He wrote many highly regarded pieces of journalism, his main talent was for drama, and he wrote more than 60 plays.

George Bernard Shaw's last words: Sister, you are trying to keep me alive as an old curiosity, but I am done. I am finished. I am going to die.

Cause of Death: Renal Failure

Buddy Rich

Born in Brooklyn, NY on September 30, 1917 – died on April 2, 1987 in Los Angeles CA. Buddy Rich was 70 years old.

Buddy Rich was an American jazz drummer and bandleader. He is widely considered one of the most influential drummers of all time.

Buddy Rich's last words: A nurse asked; Is there anything you can't take, Buddy says yea, country music.

Cause of Death: Cardiovascular disease.

Harriet Tubman

Born in Maryland on 1821 – died March 10, 1913 in Auburn, New York. Harriet was 92 years old.

Harriet Tubman was an American abolitionist and armed scout and spy for the United States during the civil war. When Harriet was dying in 1913, she gathered her family around and they sang together.

Harriet Tubman last words: singing "Swing low Sweet Chariot" This song is among the most treasured and widely recognized African American spirituals. One of the songs of the century.

Cause of Death: Pneumonia

Farrah Fawcett

Born in Corpus Christi, TX on February 2, 1947 – died on June 25, 2009 in Santa Monica, CA. Farrah Fawcett was 62 years old.

Farrah Fawcett was best known for her role as Jill Monroe on the TV series Charlies Angels in 1976. Her pin-up poster sold 12 million copies.

Farrah Fawcett's last words: She began to vomit, why aren't you filming this? This is what cancer is?

Cause of Death: Anal cancer

Sir Isaac Newton

Born in England on January 04, 1643 – died March 20, 1727 in Kensington, London, England. Isaac was 86 years old.

Isaac was a mathematician, astronomer considered the most influential scientist of all time. He said, I don't know what I may seem to the world. But as to myself, I seem to have been only like a boy playing on the seashore and diverting myself now and then in finding a smoother pebble or a prettier shell than the ordinary, whilst the great ocean of truth lay all undiscovered before me. It seems Isaac never really understood his contribution to the world, so humble a man was he.

Cause of Death: Natural causes

Oscar Wilde

Born in the Dublin, Ireland on October 16, 1854 – died on November 30, 1900. Oscar Wilde was 46 years old.

Oscar Wilde was an Irish poet and playwright. After writing in different forms throughout the 1880's, he became one of London's most popular playwrights in the early 1890's.

Oscar Wilde last words: Either that wallpaper goes, or I do. I guess he went.

Cause of Death: Meningitis

Jimmy Steward

Born in Indiana, Pennsylvania on May 20, 1908 – died on July 2, 1997 in Beverly hills, CA. Jimmy Steward was 89 years old.

Jimmy Steward an American actor and a military officer who is among the most honored and popular stars in film history.

Jimmy Stewards last words: I am going to be with Gloria now. Referring to his wife who passed three years early.

Cause of Death: Heart attack

Leonardo da Vinci

Born in Anchiano, Tuscany, Italy on April 15, 1452 – died May 2, 1519 in Clos Luce, France. Leonardo was 67 years old.

He was an inventor, painter, architecture, scientist, astronomy etc. Some of his inventions were omitaopter, parachute, viola organist, diving suit.

Leonardo da Vinci last words: I have offended God and mankind because my work did not reach the quality it should have. I guess the Mona Lisa isn't good enough?

Here is a brilliant man who thought he was never good enough. People listen to his last words. It's a message to all mankind message. You have to reach for the sky and never give up. I think we all could use a little of Leonardo's ambition and never give up attitude.

He died in the hands of the King of France.

Cause of Death: Unknown

George Reeves

Born in Woolstock, IA on January 5, 1914 – died on June 16, 1959 in Los Angeles.CA. George Reeves was 45 years old.

George Reeves was an actor. He is best known for his role as Superman in the 1950's television program Adventure of Superman.

George Reeves last words: I am tired I am going back to bed.

Cause of Death: Gunshot to the head, suicide

Karl Marx

Born in Trier, Germany on May 5, 1818 – died on March 17, 1883 in London, England. Karl Marx was 65 years old.

Karl Marx was a German philosopher, economist, sociologist, journalist and revolutionary socialist. Marx's work in economics laid the basis for much of the current understanding of labor and its relation to capital, and subsequent economic thought.

Karl Marx last words: Go on, get out-last words are for fools who haven't said enough in their life time.

Cause of Death: Bronchitis

Walt Disney

Born in Hermosa, Illinois on December 5, 1901 – died on December 15, 1966. Walt Disney was 65 years old.

Walt Disney was an American entrepreneur, animator, voice actor and film producer. A pioneer of the American animation industry. He won 26 academy awards, 3 golden globe awards.

Walt Disney's last words: Kurt Russell

Cause of Death: Lung cancer

Louise-Marie-Therese de Saint Maurice, Comtesse de Vercelli's.

Born in France September 8, 1749 – died September 3, 1792. Louise- Marie was 43 years old.

She was a confidante to Marie Antoinette and was murdered during the French Revolution.

Louise-Marie let one rip while she was dying, she said, good.

Louise-Marie last words: A woman who can fart like that is not dead. It sounds to me as if she blew the life right out of herself.

Johnny Ace

Born in Memphis, TN on June 29, 1929 – died December 25, 1954 in Houston, Texas. Johnny was 25 years old.

An R&B singer, died while playing with a pistol during a break in his concert set. **Johnny Ace last words were**, "I'll show you that it won't shoot." I guess he was wrong.

Cause of death: Self-inflicted gunshot

Richard Feynman

Born in New York on May 11, 1918 – died on February 15, 1988 in Los Angeles. Richard was 69 years old.

A physicist, author, musician, professor and traveler,

Richard Feynman last words: died saying "this dying is boring." Richard what where you expecting? Suggestions anyone?

Cause of Death: Cancer

Benjamin Franklin

Born in Boston, Mass. on January 17, 1706 – died April 17, 1790. Benjamin was 84 years old.

One of the founding fathers, author, printer, political theorist, freemason, scientist, inventor and diplomat. As Benjamin Franklin lay dying, his daughter told him to change positions so he could breathe more easily. Franklins last words were. "A dying man can do nothing easy." I think he was suggesting that; even while he was dying, his daughter still tried to control him.

Charles Lucky Luciano

Born Salvatore Lucania in Lecrae Friddi, Sicily, Italy on November 24, 1897 – died January 26, 1962 in Naples, Campania, Italy. Lucky was 64 years old. Buried in St. John's Cemetery, Queens, NY.

Lucky was considered the father of modern organized crime (Mafia) in the U.S. He was a crime boss, Gangster, Bootlegger, Human-trafficking, Drug trafficking.

Charles Luciano last words: "Tell George I want to get in the movies one way or another". His dying wish came true. His life story has been told many times in movies. He also appears as a character in HBO's Boardwalk Empire. It's a shame he never got to see his movie success.

Cause of Death: Heart attack.

Michael Landon

Born in New York City on October 31, 1936 – died on July 1, 1991 in Malibu. He was 55 years old.

Michael Landon was an American actor, writer, director and producer. He is best known for his roles as Joe Cartwright in Bonanza, Charles Ingalls in Little house on the Parrie, and Jonathan Smith in Highway to Heaven.

His family gathered around his bed, and his son said, Dad it's time to move on. **Landon last words**: "Your right. It's time. I love you all". So sad, it makes you realize death waits for no one.

Cause of Death: Cancer

Vince Lombardi

Born in Brooklyn, New York on June 11, 1913 – died in 1970. He was 57 years old.

Vince was a famed football coach and ranks first among NFL head coaches by total Championships (5). As Vince was dying he turned to his wife Marie and said:

Vince Lombardi last words: "Happy anniversary. I love you." I wonder if he really passed away, on their anniversary.

Cause of Death: Cancer

Edward R. Murrow

Born in Greensboro, North Carolina on April 25, 1908 - died April 27, 1965 in Pawling town, New York. He 57 years old.

He was a broadcast journalist and came to prominence with a series of radio broadcasts during world war two.

Edward Murrow last words to his wife Maybelle: "Snooks, will you please turn this way. I like to look at your face." What a beautiful ending.

Cause of Death: Lung cancer

Elizabeth Browning

Born in Kelloe, United Kingdom on March 6, 1806 – died on June 29, 1861 in Florence, Italy. Elizabeth Browning was 55 years old.

Elizabeth Browning was best known for her Sonnets from the Portuguese and Aurora Leigh as well as the love story between her fellow poet Robert Browning.

Elizabeth Browning last words: Her husband asked her how she was feeling today, she replied Beautiful.

Cause of Death: Drug overdose causing respiratory failure.

John Wayne

Born in Winterset, it is a city in Madison County, Iowa on May 26, 1907 – died June 11, 1979 in Los Angeles. He was 72 years old.

John Wayne's real name is Marion Mitchell Morrison. Academy award winner for true grit, John Wayne was among the top box office draws for three decades.

On June 11 with several family members surrounding him, Alissa his daughter was holding his hand and asked him if he knew who she was, in response,

John Wayne final words: of course, I know who you are. You're my girl. I love you. "Just think how life would be without family.

Cause of Death: Cancer

Ernest Hemingway

Born in oak park, Illinois on July 21, 1899 – died July 2, 1961 in Ketchum, Idaho. He was 62 years old. Ernest was an American novelist, short story writer and journalist. He won the Nobel Prize for Literature in 1954.

Before committing suicide,

Ernest Hemingway last words to his wife: "goodnight my kitten". Does this sound like someone who was about to commit suicide?

Cause of Death: Suicide

Barry White

Born in Galveston, TX on September 12, 1944 – died on July 4, 2003 in Loa Angeles. CA. Barry White was 59 years old.

Barry White was a three-time Grammy Award-winner known for his distinctive bass-baritone voice and romantic image, White's greatest success came in the 1970's as a solo singer and with The Love Unlimited Orchestra.

Barry White's last words: Leave me alone I am fine.

Cause of Death: Kidney failure

Major John Andre

Born in London, England May 2, 1750 – died October 2, 1780 in Tappan, New York. Major John Andre was 29 years old.

Major John Andre was among the most significant moments of the American Revolution. He was sentenced to die of execution before the judicial court of America after he was proven guilty of being a British spy.

The moment he was to be hanged he said:

Major John Andre last words: I pray you to bear me witness that I meet my fate like a brave man. Then he raised a white handkerchief and covered his eyes and said I am going away tonight.

Cause of Death: Hanging

Donald O'Connor

Born in Chicago on August 28, 1925 – died on September 27, 2003 in Calabasas, California. He was 78 years old.

Donald was an American dancer, singer and actor who came to fame in a series of movies with Gloria Jean, Peggy Ryan, and Francis the talking Mule. Donald with his family gathered around, he joked,

Donald O'Connor last words: "I would like to thank the Academy for my lifetime achievement award that I will eventually get." He still hasn't received one.

Cause of Death: Heart failure

Eugene O'Neill

Born in New York City on October 16, 1888 – died November 27, 1953 in Boston. Eugene O'Neill was 65 years old.

Eugene O'Neill was an American playwright and Nobel laureate in Literature.

Eugene O'Neill was born in a room at the Broadway Hotel on what is now Times Square. He died in a Boston Hotel room.

Eugene O'Neill last words: "I knew it! I knew it! Born in a Hotel room and goddamm it, dying in a hotel room.

Cause of Death: Pneumonia

Derek Jarman

Born in Northwood, England on January 31, 1942 – died February 19, 1994 in London, England. He was 52 years old. He was director and cinematographer, known for Edward the 11 (1991), Caravaggio (1986) and Wittgenstein (1993).

Derek Jarman last words: I want the world to be filled with white fluffy duckies. Does anyone see anything wrong with this last wish?

Cause of Death: AIDS

Sir Winston Churchill

Born in Woodstock, Oxford shire, England on November 30, 1874 – died January 24, 1965 in London, England. He was 90 years old.

Winston Churchill was a British stateman, army officer, and writer, who served as the Prime Minister of the United Kingdom from 1940 to 1945 and again from 1951 to 1955. Winston Churchill through his speeches during the second world war motived his countrymen to never give up while at war with Hitler.

Sir Winston Churchill also won the Nobel Prize for literature.

Sir Winston Churchill last words: I am bored with it all.

Cause of Death: Stroke

Joan Crawford

Born in San Antonio on March 23, 1904 – died May 10, 1977 in New York City. Joan was 73 years old.

She was an American film and television actress. The American Film Institute ranked Joan Crawford tenth on its list of the greatest female stars of the classic Hollywood Cinema.

Joan Crawford's last words: yelling at her housekeeper, who was praying for her. Crawford said Daman it! Don't you dare ask God to help me. Wow, need we say more about the mental state of Joan Crawford.

Cause of Death: Pancreatic cancer

Steve Jobs

Born in San Francisco on February 24, 1955 – died October 5, 2011 in Palo Alto, California. Steve was 45 years old.

Steve Jobs was an American entrepreneur, business magnate, inventor and industrial designer. He was chairman, chief executive officer, and co-founder of Apple, CEO and majority shareholder of Pixar, member of Walt Disney Company's board of directors.

Steve Jobs last words according to his sister Mona were: "Oh Wow, Oh Wow, Oh Wow."

Cause of Death: Pancreatic cancer

Alexander II of Russia

Born in Moscow, Russia on April 29, 1818 – died march 13, 1881 in St. Petersburg, Russia. Alexander was 62 years old.

Alexander was a great leader of Russia. His guards found his body mutilated lying under the seat of his carriage following a bombing and assassination plot against him.

Alexander II last words: Home to the palace to die and put out that bloody cigarette.

Cause of Death: Assassination

Dean Martin

Born in Steubenville, Ohio on June 7, 1917 – died on December 25, 1995 in Beverly Hills, California. Dean was 77 years old.

Dean Martin was an American singer, recording artist, actor, comedian and film producer.

Dean Martin last words were: I knew I shouldn't have switched from Scotch to Martinis.

Cause of Death: Cancer

Sammy Davis Jr.

Born in New York city on December 8, 1925 – died on May 16, 1990 in Beverly Hills, California.

Sammy Davis Jr. was an American singer, dancer, actor and comedian. Sammy Davis was part of the rat pack with Frank Sinatra and Dean Martin.

Sammy Davis Jr. last words: To his adopted son, you are my real son. Found out later his adopted son was his blood son, a love child from an affair.

Cause of Death: Esophageal cancer

Emily Dickinson

Born in Monson, Massachusetts on December 10, 1830 – died on May 15, 1886 in Amherst, Mass. Emily was 56 years old.

Emily Dickinson was a famous American poet. She wrote over 1800 poems, and fewer than a dozen was published over her lifetime.

Emily Dickinson last words: I must go in, for the fog is rising.

Cause of Death: Bright's disease/high blood pressure.

James Brown

Born on May 3, 1933 in Barnwell, South Carolina – died on December 25, 2006 in Atlanta, Georgia. James was 73 years old.

James Brown was an American singer, songwriter, dancer, musician, record producer and bandleader.

James Brown last words: I am going away tonight and he did.

Cause of Death: Pneumonia

Truman Capote

Born in New Orleans on September 30, 1924 _- died on August 25, 1984 in Los Angeles, California. Truman was 59 years old.

Truman Capote was a best-selling author. He was a pioneering force in publishing who became lost in the celebrity world.

Truman Capote last words were: He constantly repeated, Mama, Mama, Mama.

Cause of Death: Liver disease and multiple drug intoxication

General John Sedgewick

Born in Cornwall, Connecticut on September 13, 1813 – died May 9, 1864 in Spotsylvania county, VA. He was 50 years old.

John Sedgewick was a career military officer and a union General in the civil war. He was the highest-ranking officer to be killed in the civil war.

John Sedgewick Last words: They couldn't hit an elephant at this distance. Then he was shot.

Cause of Death: Firearm

Errol Flynn

Born in Hobart, Australia on June 20, 1909 – died October 14, 1959 in Vancouver, Canada. Errol Flynn was 50 years old.

Errol Flynn was an American actor, writer, film producer and famous for his romantic swashbuckler roles in Hollywood films.

Errol Flynn's last words: I've had a hell of a lot of fun and I have enjoyed every minute of it.

Cause of Death: Heart attack.

Bill Paxton

Born in Fort Worth, TX on May 17, 1955 – died on February 25, 2017 in Cedars-Sinai Medical Center, Los Angeles, CA. Bill Paxton was 61 years old.

Bill Paxton was an American actor and director. He appeared in films such as the Terminator.

Bill Paxton's last words: Thanks for all the good wishes, it will help me face this ordeal.

Cause of Death: Stroke

Charlie Chaplain

Born in London, United Kingdom on April 16, 1889 – died on December 25, 1977 in Vaud, Switzerland. Charlie Chaplain was 88 years old.

Charlie Chaplain was known for his character "The Tramp" the sweet little man with a bowler hat, mustache and cane, Charlie Chaplin was an iconic figure of the silent film era and one of film's superstars.

Charlie Chaplin's last words: The priest said have mercy on your soul, Chaplin replied, Why not? After all it belongs to him.

Cause of Death: Stroke

Ludwig Van Beethoven

Born December 1770 in Born, Germany – died March 26, 1827 in Vienna, Austria. He was 56 years old.

Ludwig was a German composer and pianist. A crucial figure in the transition between the Classical and the Romantic eras in Western music. He remains one of the most famous and influential composers of all time.

Ludwig van Beethoven last words: Friends applaud, the comedy is over.

Cause of Death: Hepatitis cirrhosis of the liver.

Roger Ailes

Born in Warren, Ohio on May 15, 1940 – died on May 18, 2017 in Palm Beach, Fl. Roger Ailes was 77 years old.

Roger Ailes transformed the cable news landscape during his reign as chief of the Fox news channel from 1996 to 2016.

Roger Ailes last words: Trump is guilty.

Cause of Death: Subdural hematoma

Sigmund Freud

Born in Pribor, Czech Republic on May 6, 1856 – died on September 23, 1939 in Hampstead, United Kingdom. Sigmund Freud was 83 years old.

Sigmund Freud was known for Psychoanalysis and was the first to use this term in 1896. Freud's theories blossomed and the terms unconscious, conscious, or conscience. Which developed into ID, Ego, Superego.

Sigmund Freud last words: This is absurd, this is absurd.

Cause of Death: Drug overdose.

Philip Seymore Hoffman

Born in New York City, NY. on July 23, 1967 – died on February 2, 2014 in New York City, NY. Philip Seymore Hoffman was 56 years old.

Philip Seymore Hoffman was known for films such as Scent of a Woman, Boogie Nights, The Big Lebowski and Capote, for which he won an Academy Award.

Philip Seymore Hoffman's last words: If one of us dies of an overdose 10 people who were about to won't.

Cause of Death: Drug overdose

O. Henry

Born in Greensboro, North Carolina on September 11, 1862 – died on June 5, 1910. Henry was 48 years old.

William Sydney Porter, known by his pen name O. Henry was an American short story writer. His stories are known for their surprise endings.

Henry's last words: Turn up the lights. I don't want to go home in the dark.

Cause of Death: Cirrhosis of the liver

John Lennon

Born in Liverpool. United Kingdom on October 9, 1940 – died on December 8, 1980. John Lennon was 40 years old.

John Lennon was a singer, songwriter who co-founded the Beatles which was one of the most commercially successful band in the history of music and sold more records than any other band in history.

John Lennon's last words: He was asked in the hospital after being shot, are you John Lennon. John said: Yes, I am. Last words.

Cause of Death: Gunshot-murdered

Kit Carson

Born in Madison county, Kentucky on December 24, 1809 – died May 23, 1868 in Fort Lyon, Co. He was 58 years old.

Kit Carson was an American frontiers man, mountain man, wilderness guide, Indian agent and American Army officer.

Kit Carson's last words: Wish I had time for just one more bowl of chili

Cause of Death: Abdominal aortic aneurysm

Amelia Earhart

Born in Atchison, KS on July 24, 1897 – disappeared on July 2, 1937 over the Pacific Ocean. Amelia Earhart was 39 years old.

Amelia Earhart was an American aviator pioneer and author. Earhart was the first female aviator to fly solo across the Atlantic Ocean. Shae received the United states distinguished flying cross.

Amelia Earhart Last words: KHAQQ calling Itasca. We must be on you Gas is running low.

Cause of Death: Plane crash

Marilyn Monroe

Born in Los Angeles, CA. on June 1. 1926 – died August 5, 1962 in Los Angeles, CA. Marilyn Monroe was 36 years old.

Marilyn Monroe was the original blonde bombshell, she went from modelling to acting, generally playing the dumb blonde. Remembered for singing Happy Birthday to President John F. Kennedy.

Marilyn Last words: Say goodbye to Pat, goodbye to Jack and say goodbye to yourself because you are a nice guy. She was making reference to JFK.

Cause of Death: Drug overdose

Rock Hudson

Born in Winnetka, Illinois on November 17, 1925 – died on 2, 1985 in Beverly hills, ca. Rock Hudson was 60 years old.

Rock Hudson was an American actor, generally known for his turns as a leading man during the 1950's and 60's.

Rock Hudson's last words: No, I don't think so. I wonder who he was talking to?

Cause of Death: Aids

Cary Grant

Born in Hopfield, Bristol, England on January 18, 1904 – died November 29, 1986 in davenport, Iowa. Cary Grant was 82 years old., known as one of the classic holly

Cary Grant was an English-American actor, who acted in over 76 films named the second greatest male star of the golden era Humphrey bogart was the first.

Cary Grant's last words: I love you, Barber, don't worry.

Cause of Death: intracerebral hemorrhage

Ava Gardner

Born in Grab town, North Carolina on December 24, 1922 – died January 25, 1990 in London, England. Ava Gardner was 67 years old.

Ava Gardner was an American actress and singer. She is listed among the American film Institute's 25 greatest female stars of classic Hollywood.

Ava Gardner's last words: I am so tried.

Cause of Death: Pneumonia

John Wilkes Booth

Born in Bel Air, MD. on May 10, 1838 – died on April 26, 1865 Port Royal, VA. John Wilkes Booth was 27 years old.

John Wilkes Booth was an American actor who assassinated President Abraham Lincoln on April 14, 1965.

John Wilkes Booth last words: Useless, Useless, Useless.

Cause of Death: Gunshot wound

Chuck Berry

Born in St. Louis, MO. On October 18, 1926 – died on March 18, 2017 in Wentzville, MO. Chuck Berry was 90 years old.

Chuck Berry was a song writer and guitarist who was one of the most popular and influential performers in rock & roll.

Chuck Berry's last words: I would kick that f...... gambling and drug addict Pete Rose in the balls and toss his limp body in the river.

Cause of Death: Cardiac arrest

Bob Marley

Born in Nine Mile Jamaica on February 6, 1945 – died on May 11, 1981 in Miami. Bob Marley was 36 years old.

Bob Marley popularize reggae around the world. He was a song writer who could mix protest music and pop as well as Bob Dylan.

Bob Marley's last words: Money can't buy life.

Cause of Death: Cancer

Bruce Lee

Born in San Francisco, CA. on November 27, 1940 – died on July 20, 1973 in Kowloon Tong, Hong Kong. Bruce Lee was 33 years old.

Bruce Lee was inspirational in bringing Martial Arts to the world. He was a revered Martial artist, actor and filmmaker known for movies like fist of fury and enter the Dragon.

Bruce's Lees last words: Enter the dragon and the martial arts explosion.

Cause of Death: Cerebral Edema

Jim Morrison

Born in Melbourne, Fl. On December 8, 1943 – died on July 3, 1971 in Paris, France. Jim Morrison was 27 years old.

Jim Morrison was a singer and songwriter with the group the doors which he left in 1971 to write poetry in Paris France.

Jim Morrison's last words: Last words, Last words out.

Cause of Death: Heart failure

Janis Joplin

Born in Port Arthur, TX on January 19, 1943 – died on October 4, 1970 in Hollywood, CA. Janis Joplin was 26 years old.

Janis Joplin was known for her powerful blues inspired voice. Her nickname was first lady of rock and roll.

Janis Joplin last words: Get it while you can.

Cause of Death: Heroin overdose

Jimi Hendrix

Born in Seattle, WA. On November 27, 1942 – died on September 18, 1970 in London, England. Jimi Hendrix was 28 years old.

Jimi Hendrix was known as the world's greatest guitar player.

Jimi Hendrix last words: I need help man.

Cause of Death: Drug overdose

Kurt Cobain

Born in Aberdeen, WA. On February 20, 1967 – died on April 5, 1994 in Seattle, WA. Kurt Cobain was 27 years old.

Kurt Cobain started the grunge band Nirvana in 1988 and made the leap to a major record label.

Kurt Cobain's last words: It's better to burn out than fade out.

Cause of Death: Suicide

Corey Haim

Born in Toronto, Canada on December 23, 1971 – died on March 10, 2010 in Burbank, CA. Cory Haim was 38 years old.

Corey Haim was an actor and starred in a number of movies such as Lucas, Silver Bullet, Murphy's Romance, License to drive Etc.

Corey Haim's last words: Doing really well.

Cause of Death: Drug overdose

Desi Arnaz

Born in Santiago, Cuba on march 2, 1917 – died on December 2, 1986 in Del Mar. CA. Desi Arnaz was 69 years old.

Desi Arnaz was an American actor, musician and producer. He brought I love Lucy TV series to the market place. Lucille Ball and Desi formed their own production company.

Desi Arnaz last words: I love you honey, Good luck with your show.

Cause of Death: Lung cancer

Lucille Ball

Born in Jamestown, New York on august 6, 1911 – died on April 26, 1989 in Los Angeles, ca. Lucille Ball was 77 years old.

Lucille Ball was an American actress, comedian, model, film studio executive and producer. Best known for the" I Love Lucy show"

Lucille Ball's last words: Florida water. I wonder what she meant by that?

Cause of Death: abdominal aortic dissection

Humphrey Bogart

Born in New York, New York on December 25, 1899 - died on January 14, 1957 in Los Angeles, CA. Humphrey Bogart was 57 years old.

Humphrey Bogart was a distinguished Hollywood actor. He was a top box-office attraction during the 1940's and 50's. Humphrey Bogart became a cult hero of the America cinema.

Humphrey's last words were: Goodbye Kid. Hurry back.

Cause of Death: Esophagus cancer

Steve Irwin

Born in Essendon, Australia on February 22, 1962 – died on September 4, 2006 in the Batt, Australia. Steve Irwin was 43 years old.

Steve Irwin was a wildlife expert and part entertainer, Irwin became world famous for his TV series. The Crocodile Hunter.

Steve Irwin last worst: I am dying.

Cause of Death: Stingray injury.

The Last words of Saints.

As the Saints embraced martyrdom, many of the Saints quoted scripture, while others were defiant and some provided messages for their followers.

The following is last the words from some of the Saints. See if there is a message that resonates with you.

Jesus Christ

Born in Bethlehem died at the age of 33 years old.

Cause of death crucifixion.

The last words of Jesus on the cross.

Father, forgive them, for they do not know what they do.

Truly. I say to you, today you will be with me in Paradise.

Jesus said to his Mother: Woman. This is your son. Then he said to the disciple: This is your mother.

My God, my God, why have you forsaken me?

"I thirst"

When Jesus had received the wine, he said, it is finished: and bowed his head and handed over his spirit.

Jesus cried out in a loud voice. Father, into your hands I commend my spirit.

St. Andrew (Martyr)

Born in Galilee, Israel in 5 BC - died November 30, 60 AD in Patras, Achaia, (Greece) one of the twelve apostles of Jesus and brother of St. Peter. St. Andrew was 65 years old.

St. Andrews last words:

Lord, eternal King of glory, receive me hanging from the wood of this sweet cross. Thou art my God, whom I have seen, do not permit them to loosen me from this cross. Do this for me. O lord for I know the virtue of the holy cross.

Cause of Death: Crucifixion

St. Andrew Kim Taegon (Martyr)

Born in Dangjin, South Korea on august 21, 1821 – died on September 16, 1846 in Seoul, South Korea. St. Andrew Kim Taegon was 25 years old.

St. Andrew Kim Taegon last words:

This is my last hour of life, listen to me attentively: if I have held communication with foreigners, it has been for my religion and for my God. It is for him that I die. My immortal life is on the point of beginning. Become Christians if you wish to be happy after death, because God has eternal chastisements in store for those who refused to know him.

Cause of Death: Murder

St. Augustine

Born in Thagaste, Numidia on November 13, 354 AD. – died on August 28, 430 AD. in Hippo Regius, Algeria. St. Augustine was 75 years old.

His writings influenced the development of western Christianity and western philosophy.

St. Augustine's last words: Your will be done. Come, Lord Jesus

Cause of Death: Unknown

St. Bartholomew

Born in Cana at Galilee – Died near Albano polis, Armenia.

St. Bartholomew was one of the twelve apostles of Jesus.

St. Bartholomew last words: My only desire is to see Mary who saved me and who will save me from the clutches of Satan.

Cause of death: Skinned alive, he was flayed alive the skin of his body cut into strips then pulled off, then beheaded.

St. Bernadette Sourbirous

Born in Lourdes, France on January 7, 1844 – died on April 16, 1879 in Nevers, France. St. Bernadette Sourbirous was 35 years old.

St. Bernadette was best known as the Saint who received visions from the Virgin Mary in a cave near Lourdes, France.

St. Bernadette last words: Holy Mary, pray for me, a poor sinner.

Cause of Death: Tuberculosis

St. Catherine of Siena

Born in Siena, Italy on march 25, 1347 – died on April 29, 1380 in Rome, Italy. St. Catherine was 33 years old.

St. Catherine was a tertiary of the Dominican order and a scholastic philosopher and theologian. She worked to bring the papacy of Gregory X1 back to Rome from France.

St. Catherine's last words: Blood! Blood! Father, into Thy hands I commend my spirit.

Cause of Death: Stroke

St. Clelia Barbieri

Born in bologna, Italy on February 13, 1847 – died on July 13, 1870 in Persiceto, Italy. St. Clelia Barbieri was 22 years old.

St. Clelia Barbieri was an Italian Roman Catholic and founder of the Little Sisters of the Mother of Sorrows.

St. Clelia Barbieri last words: Be brave, because I am going to Paradise; but I shall always remain with you, too, I shall never abandon you!

Cause of Death: Tuberculosis

St. David

Born in Pembroke shire, Wales in 520 - died march 1, 601 in St. David's, United Kingdom. St. David was about 80 years old, no one knows for sure.

St. David is the patron saint of wales. During the battle with the Saxons he had the Welsh place a leek on their helmet so you could tell who the was enemy. The Welsh won the battle.

St. David's last words: Be joyful and keep the faith and your creed. Do the little things that you have seen me do and heard about. I will walk the path that our fathers have trod before us.

Cause of Death: Natural causes

St. Elizabeth Ann Seton

Born in New York City, NY on august 28, 1774 – died January 4, 1821 in Emmitsburg, MD. St. Elizabeth Ann Seton was 46 years old.

St. Elizabeth Ann Seton was the first native born citizen of the United States to be canonized by the Roman Catholic Church. The daughters of charity trace their origins to Elizabeth Ann Seton.

St. Elizabeth Ann Seton last words: Be children of the church.

Cause of Death: Tuberculosis

St. Faustina Kowalska

Born in Glogowiec, Poland on August 25, 1905 – died October 5, 1938 in Krakow, Poland. St. Faustina Kowalska was 33 years old. I am thoroughly enwrapped in God.

St. Faustina Kowalsa had a vision of Jesus Christ where she was instructed to draw a picture of him showing the rays of red and pale blue radiating from his chest.

St. Faustina Kowalsa last words:

Today the Majesty of God is surrounding me. There is no way that I can help myself prepare better. My soul is being inflamed by his love. I only know that I love and am loved. That is enough for me. I am trying my best to be faithful throughout the day to the Holy Spirit and to fulfill his demands. I am trying my best for interior silence to be able to hear his voice.

Cause of Death: Tuberculosis

St. Francis of Assisi

Born in Assisi, Italy between December 1181 and September 1182 – died on October 3, 1226 in Assisi, Italy. St. Francis Assisi was 44 years old.

St. Francis of Assisi was founder of the Franciscan Order.

St. Francis of Assisi last words:

When you see that I am brought to my last moments, place me naked upon the ground just as you saw me the day before yesterday; and let me lie there after I am dead for the length of time it takes one to walk a mile unhurriedly.

Cause of Death: He was seriously ill and Stigmata appeared on his body matching those recorded on Jesus after his crucifixion.

St. John the Baptist

Born in Jerusalem, Israel around 5 BC. – died 28-29 AD in Machaerus, Jordan. John the Baptist was about 33 years old.

St. John the Baptist was the one who Baptized Jesus in the river Jordan.

St. John the Baptist last words: In all things I adore the will of God in my regard.

Cause of Death: Beheaded

St. Joan of Arc (Martyr)

Born in Domremy, Bar, France in 1412 – Died on May 30, 1431 in Rouen. St. Joan of Arc was 19 years old.

St. Joan of Arc was the national heroine of France, at age 18 she led the French army to victory over the English at Orleans. She was captured a years later and burned at the stake.

St. Joan of Arc last words: Jesus, Jesus, Jesus

Cause of Death: Smoke inhalation

St. John Chrysostom

Born in Antioch, Syria in 347 – died on September 14, 407 in Commana, Helenopontus.

St. John Chrysostom has made exhaustive commentaries on the divine Scriptures and was the author of more works than any other church father with over 1440 sermons alone.

St. John Chrysostom last words: Let me go to the house of the Father.

Cause of Death: Unspecified

St. John Paul the Great

Born in Wadowice, Poland on May 18, 1920 – died on April 2, 2005 in Apostolic Palace, Vatican City. St. John Paul was 85 years old.

St. John Paul was pope from 1978 to 2005. He was the first non-Italian to be pope in more than 400 years.

St. John Paul brought the public back to religion and the Catholic Church. He was the people's Pope and was loved by everyone whether they were Catholic or not.

St. John Paul last words: Let me go to the house of my father.

Cause of Death: Septic shock

St. Laurence (Martyr)

Born in Hispania, Spain on December 31, 225 AD – died on August 10, 258 ADS in Rome, Italy. St. Laurence was 32 years old.

St. Laurence was a Roman Deacon under Pope Saint Sixtus II. Four days after his death the Pope was put to death by Emperor Valerian.

St. Laurence last words

O Christ, only God, O Splendor, O power of the Father, O Maker of the Heaven and earth builder of this city's walls. Thou have placed Rome's scepter high over all; Thou hast willed to subject the world to it, in order to unite under one law, the nations which differ in manners, customs, language, genius and sacrifice. Behold the whole human race has submitted to its empire, and all discord and dissensions disappear in its unity. Remember thy purpose: Thou didst will to bind the immense universe together into one Christian Kingdom. O Christ, for the sake of thy Romans, make this city Christian; for to it Thou gravest the charge of leading all the rest to sacred unity. All its members in every place are united-a very type of Thy Kingdom; the conquered universe has bowed before it. Oh! May its royal head have bowed in turn! Send Gabriel and bid him heal the blindness of the sons of Iulus, that they may know the true God. I see a prince who is to come-an Emperor who is a servant of God. He will suffer Rome to remain a slave; he will close the temples and fasten them with bolts forever. **Death Execution**

St. Stephen (Martyr)

Born in 5 AD – died 34 AD in Jerusalem, Israel. St. Stephen was 29 years old.

St. Stephen was the first Martyr of Christianity, according to Acts of the Apostles, a deacon in the early church who aroused various Synagogues by his teachings.

St. Stephens last words: Lord Jesus receive my spirit, Lord, lay not this sin to their charge. (Addressed to his executioners)

Cause of Death: Stoning

St. Thomas Becket (Martyr)

Born in London, England in December 21, 1118 – died on December 29, 1170 in Canterbury, England. St. Thomas Becket was 52 years old.

St. Thomas Becket was the Archbishop of Canterbury from 1162 to 1170. He refused to give the monarchy power over the church.

St. Thomas Becket last words: If all the swords in England were pointed at my head, your threats would not move me. I am ready to die for my lord, that in my blood the Church may obtain liberty and peace. (spoken to his murders)

Cause of Death: Assassination

St. Thomas More (Martyr)

Born in London, England on February 7, 1478 – died on July 6, 1535 in London, England. St. Thomas More was 53 years old.

St. Thomas More was known for his book Utopia and for refusing to acknowledge King Henry the 8th as the head of the church of England.

St. Thomas Mores last words: I die the King's servant but God's first.

Cause of Death: Decapitation

Criminals

Thomas Grasso

Born in Tulsa, ok on November 23, 1962 – died on March 20, 1995 in McAlester, Ok. He was 33 years old.

Convicted murderer used is last words to complain about his last meal.

Thomas Grasso last words: "I did not get my Spaghetti-O's. I got spaghetti". I want the press to know. I bet the press ate this one up.

Cause of Death: Execution

Carl Panzram

Born in Grande Forks, Minnesota on June 28, 1892 – died on September 5, 1930 in Leavenworth, KS. Carl Panzram was 38 years old.

Carl Panzram was a serial killer, rapist, arsonist who confessed to 22 murders and to having sodomized over 1,000 males, adding for all these things I am not in the least bit sorry.

Carl Panzram last words: As the noose was placed around his neck, I wish the entire human race had one neck, and I had my hands around it.

Cause of Death: Hanging

John Arthur Spenkelink

Born in Le Mars, Ia on March 29,1949 - and died on May 25, 1979 in Raiford, Fl. John Spenkelink was 29 years old.

John Spenkelelink was a convicted American murderer. Before he was executed he spent his final days writing on anything it could. Capital punishment means: **John Arthur Spenkelink last words**: "those without capital get the punishment". I have to admit he is right on this one.

Cause of Death: Execution

Mary Elizabeth Jenkins Surratt

Born in waterloo, Maryland in May of 1823 – died July 7, 1865 in Washington Penitentiary. Mary Surratt was 42 years old.

Mary Surratt was the first woman to have ever been executed by the military tribunal of the Federal Government. She was executed in public on July 7, 1865 guilty of treason. She was also involved in the conspiracy to assassinate the late US president Abraham Lincoln. This was obvious krama for her.

Mary Surratt last words: Please don't let me fall.

Cause of Death: Hanging

Gary Gilmore

Born in McCamey, TX on December 4, 1940 – died on January 17, 1977 in Draper, UT. Gary Gilmore was 36 years old.

Gary Gilmore was a convicted Utah murderer who was demanding his own death. Gary Gilmore had killed two people in two days during the summer of 1976.

He became the first person to be executed after the U.S. reinstated the death penalty.

Gary Gilmore's last words: Just Do It!

Cause of Death: Firing squad

Gary's last words were the inspiration for Nike's tagline, "Just Do It".

So now you know the rest of the story.

James D. French

Born in 1936 – died August 10, 1966 in Oklahoma. James French 29 years old.

James French was a criminal who was the last person to be executed under Oklahoma's death penalty laws. He was the only prisoner to be executed in the U.S. that year.

French wanted to died but was afraid to kill himself so, French killed his cellmate apparently to compel the state to execute him.

James D. French last words: "How's this for a headline? "French Fries."

Cause of death: The electric chair

Aileen Wuornos

Born in Rochester, MI on February 29, 1956 – died on October 9, 2002 in Starke, Fl. Aileen Wuornos was 46 years old.

Aileen Wuornos was a serial killer who had killed seven men, widely believed to be the first female serial killer.

Aileen Wuornos last words: Yes, I would just like to say I am sailing with the rock, and I will be back, like independence with Jesus, June 6, like the movie with a big mother ship and all. I will be back.

Cause of Death: Capital Punishment

Saddam Hussein

Born in Al-Awja, Iraq on April 28, 1937 – died on December 30, 2006 in Bagdad, Iraq. Saddam Hussein was 68 years old.

Saddam Hussein was president of Iraq from July 16, 1979 until the 9th of April 2003. Under his rule, segments of the populace enjoyed the benefits of the oil wealth, while those in opposition faced torture and execution.

Saddam Hussein last words: There is no God but Allah and Muhammad are God's messenger.

Cause of Death: Hanging

Karla Faye Brown

Born in Houston, TX on November 18, 1959 – died on February 3, 1998 in Huntsville, TX. Karla Faye Brown was 39 years old.

Karla Faye Brown was sentenced to death for murdering two people in cold blood during a robbery.

Karla Faye Brown's last words: I am going to face to face with Jesus. I love you all very much. I will see you when I get there. I will wait for you.

Cause of Death: Capital Punishment.

Johnny Frank Garrett

Born in Texas on December 24, 1963 – died on February 11, 1992 in Huntsville, Texas. Johnny was 28 years old.

Johnny Frank Garrett was accused of raped and strangled a 76-year-old nun. Evidence has come to light proving Johnny Frank Garrett was innocent. Another case of an overzealous prosecutor.

Johnny Frank Garrett last words: I would like to thank my family for loving and taking care of me and the rest of the world can kiss my ass.

Cause of Death: Capital Punishment.

Ted Bundy

Born in Burlington, VT on November 24, 1946 – died on January 24, 1989 in Florida. Ted Bundy was 42 years old.

Ted Bundy was a 1970's serial murderer, rapist and necrophiliac. Ted Bundy admitted to killing 36 women but, they believe it could be over 100.

Ted Bundy's last words: I would like to give my love to family and friend's.

Cause of Death: Capital Punishment.

Robert Alton Harris

Born in Fort Bragg, NC on January 15, 1953 – died on April 21, 1992 in San Quentin State Prison. Robert Alton Harris was 39 years old.

Robert Alton Harris was a murderer, kidnapper, burglary, robber. He murdered two teenage boys in 1978.

Robert Alton Harris last words: You can be a king or a street sweeper, but everyone dances with the grim reaper.

Cause of death: The gas chamber/capital punishment

Christopher Scott Emmett

Born in Virginia on August 18, 1971 – died on July 24, 2008 in Waverly, Virginia. Christopher Scoot Emmett was 36 years old.

Christopher Scott Emmett was convicted of murder and robbery of his co-worker.

Christopher Scott Emmett's last words: Tell my family I love them, tell the Governor he just lost my vote. You all hurry this along I am dying to get out of here.

Cause of Death: Capital Punishment

John Wayne Gacy

Born in Chicago, IL on March 17, 1942 – died on may 10, 1994 in Crest Hill, Il. John Wayne Gacy was 52 years old.

John Wayne Gacy was a serial killer and rapist. He sexually assaulted, tortured and murdered at least 33 teenage boys and young men between 1972 and 1978.

John Wayne Gacy last words: Kiss my ass.

Cause of Death: Capital punishment.

Dutch Schultz

Born in the Bronx, New York City, NY on August 6, 1902 – died on October 24, 1935 in Newark, NJ. Dutch Schultz was 33 years old.

Dutch Schultz was a mobster of the 1920s and 1930s who made his fortune in organized crime-related activities, including bootlegging and the numbers racket. He was killed by members of the notorious hit squad "Murder Inc".

Everyone was fearful of Dutch Schultz, no one could control him.

Dutch Schultz last words: As he laid dying; Shut up, you got s big mouth! Henry. Max, come over here…. French Canadian bean soup…I want to pay. Let them leave me alone.

Cause of Death: Murdered

Jeffery Dahmer

Born in Milwaukee, WI on May 21, 1960 – died on November 28, 1994 in Columbia Correctional Institution in Portage, WI. Jeffery Dahmer was 34 years old.

Jeffery Dahmer also known as the Milwaukee Cannibal was an American serial killer and sex offender, who committed the rape, murder and dismemberment of 17 men and boys from 1978 to 1991.

Rumor has it that when they caught Jeffery Dahmer he was cooking body parts on the stove.

Jeffery Dahmer's last words: I don't care if I live or die, go ahead and kill me.

Cause of Death: Capital punishment

William Bonin

Born in Willimantic, CT on January 8, 1947 – died on February 23, 1996 in San Quentin State Prison, San Quentin, CA. William Bonin was 49 years old.

William Bonin was a serial killer and twice-paroled sex offender, also know as the freeway killer, who committed rape, torture and murder of a minimum of 21 boys.

William Bonin last words: I would suggest that when a person has a thought of doing anything serious against the law, that before they do that they should go to a quiet place and think about it.

Cause of Death: Capital Punishment

Kenneth McDuff

Born in Rosebud, TX on March 21, 1946 – died on November 17, 1998 in Huntsville, TX. Kenneth McDuff was 41 years old.

Kenneth McDuff was a serial killer responsible for 14 plus murders.

Kenneth McDuff last words: I am ready to be released. Release me.

Cause of Death: Capital punishment

Random Last Words Stories

The Jesus Story

His mother tried to make her son accept Jesus into his heart.

He would tell her to F...k off. The family remained bedside. The last day he was very angry. The family called the nurse in because they thought he wasn't responding, (shallow breaths, glossy eyes, and cold skin the end was imminent) His lovely mother, in her dearest attempt, whispered to him to go towards the light, to her Jesus. With his dying breath he opened his eyes, looked at her and said F....K your Jesus !!!. A second or two later, he slowly turned his head to the left, and got the most horrific look on his face as if he was looking at something we couldn't see, and horrified, like in a bad movie, his face contorted, and he screamed with his last breath, eyes wide, OH shit, oh shit OH NOOOOOO!!!!!. Then made a guttural noise and promptly fell back into bed and died. Every family was shaking and too frightened to speak.

"Frank, Frank, here I come. Oh, honey I have missed you so much!"

My grandmother died in 1999 my grandfather died in 1975. She never remarried, never dated, but lived a great life. When she was dying she yelled. "Frank, Frank, come here, oh honey I have missed you so much, where have you been, take me with you. Then she died.

"It's about damn time you got here! I have been waiting!"

My mother was watching over my grandfather in the hospital. He had been unresponsive for a day or so, when suddenly he said: "It's about damn time you got here! I have been waiting! And then he died."

"Kill me"

A cancer patient was on high dose of morphine and hallucinating, she would alternate between grasping for things not there and trying to climb out of bed. She was too unsteady to walk, so my job was to sit in the room and make sure it was safe, she tried to get up and I asked her what she needed. She gripped my arm and pulled me down towards her face and said, very angrily, he is going to kill me. Then moments later she died.

"The old grey mare ain't what she used to be."

Checked in on a patient before the end of my shift and she was in a good frame of mind. She was telling me stories the whole time. Her condition was terminal. I asked her how she was doing and she said "the old grey mare ain't what she used to be. "And won't be here in the morning. She had died overnight.

"Bills here, love, I have got to go."

While student nurse I was caring for a terminally ill patient. She was talking away, when all of a sudden she stopped, looked over my shoulder and said, "Bill is here, love, I have to go now and immediately stopped breathing and died. We found out later Bill was her dead husband.

"There are actual angels who keep coming into my room."

I went to visit a friend of mine who was terminal ill. It so happened it was the last day of his life. He was a kind of no bull shit kind of guy. He leaned over and said to me, Bob there have been angels in my room, on and off all day. I asked him if the pain killer he was on could be making him see the angels. He said no way. There are actual angels that just keep coming in my room. I asked him if he was afraid, he said know they have come to take me with them. Shortly after I left he passed away.

"I am going to see you again, brother."

My grandfather's brother, had died six hours after my grandfather and minutes before he said, "I am going to see you again, brother."

He didn't know at the time that my grandfather (his brother) had died. The family was going to tell him the next morning because he was having a bad day.

"The Devil has been in my room all night, but don't worry, God is with you.'

The devil has been in my room all night but don't worry, God is with You. This man must have had the worst death ever. He had a horrendous seizure and died with his eyes wide open and a horrible grimace of fear on his face. He had been yelling about the Devil over and over again. Telling the devil to get out of here.

"Why are they here."

My grandmother when dying told her daughter, no I don't want to go and kept asking her daughter why all these people are here. Then my grandmother realized they were there for her and shortly died.

"Tomorrow I will be dead."

When my grandmother was dying someone had to stay with her all day. One night my cousin volunteered to sit with her. The house she lived in was creepy, the lights from the family room didn't reach the stairs or the hallway. Around 1 am my grandmother starts making faces at the stairs and when my cousin asks what's wrong, my grandmother, "I just wish the man on the stairs will quit starring at us." Then my cousin mentions how more family members will be arriving the next day. My grandmother said it doesn't matter I won't be here by morning and she wasn't.

My Thoughts on Saying Goodbye

1) Saying goodbye to a loved one is one of the most difficult things we have do in life. But avoiding the subject and meaningful conversations with the dying is the number one source of regret. People try to time the death of a loved one so they can be there is next to impossible. The dying seems to have the ability to choose the moment of death. It is quite common for them to spare those they love by waiting until those people leave the room.

   Dying people want to hear four main things from their loved ones, "Please forgive me," I forgive you," Thank you," I love you."

2) We all seem to avoid the topic of death when we visit a dying loved one. But you must realize they are fully aware of what's going on and when you don't talk about it, it's like a big elephant in the room.

3) If the loved ones talk directly about death, go along, don't say, no you're not dying. It's like trying to argue with a woman in labor. Help your loved one see that they made a difference in the world or in the family. They need to feel their life had meaning or purpose.

4) It's important, if your loved one is in a comma to keep on talking. Hearing is the last sense to go and you have to assume your loved one can hear you.

5) Be in the moment, so many of us are always looking to what we are doing next. Stay present with your loved one in the moment. It's the most important thing you can do. The office can wait.

6) There is no right way or wrong way to behave. For some people it may be telling jokes, don't feel you have to be somber.

7) Don't feel every time you visit you have to have a final goodbye. Not knowing if it's the final one brings the best visits to an uncertain situation. You can say your goodbye's many ways in many visits. It's important when leaving to let your loved one know you love them.

8) Finally, just showing up is the most important thing, you can speak in volumes without speaking a word. or just stroking an arm or shoulder. Smiles and kisses.

My Conclusion about the Last Words Of the Dying

What happens when we die, where do we go, who do we see. We will never truly know the answers to these questions until we die ourselves. But in our last moments of life, do the dying get a glimpse at what may be in store for them on the other side.

A national survey of individuals who work with the dying have revealed some very interesting findings on what the dying may see, hear or feel during their last moments.

As their body begins the process of totally shutting down. The dying is at the threshold between life and death.

Those who work with the dying, witnessing their final moments, state most of the time that the dying will hear voices of loved ones, returning to call them home, they may hear music, they may see their favorite places they have visited. Sometimes the dying will reach-up for family members that have passed away.

Others report seeing angels and feeling the presence of God. There is a world out there that the dying sees. We the living are unable to see through the vail that connects life and death.

Family members that have died, will talk to the dying letting them know not to be afraid, you're not alone we are here. This brings the dying much needed comfort.

Sometimes what can make saying goodbye so difficult is the drugs and pain that people suffer during this time. This undermines their ability to interact with their family in a coherent way.

Another one is how many people die alone, with no one there at the time of death to hear their last words.

Medical science claims they have an answer for these situations, which may be the hallucinations of the dying brain, but these conversations and visits from the other side are real to the dying.

There are lessons in this for all of us, from the dying to the living. Do something nice for someone today, there may not be a tomorrow.

It is never too late to say your sorry or to tell someone you love them. No matter how many years has pasted or how difficult the situation may have been.

What matters is relationships, our relations with the people we love is really all we have at the end of our lives.

I use this analogy about the end of our life, imagine getting onto an airplane, as you get on the airplane, people are crying, waving saying goodbye.

As the airplane takes off and lands at another location, there are people there waiting, crying, waving and saying, what took you so long to get here.

I truly wish for my scenario of the transition from life to death is accurate. But we will never really know until we die!

Finally, there is no doubt that the last words of the dying can be of great importance to the dying person and others. The interest in last words can have both positive and negative influences for the living.

Positive because it might encourage continued visits with the dying, and negative because by placing to much importance on the final words, instead of being there for the whole dying process, may not be in the best interest of the dying.

About the Author

Douglas Casimiri was born in Toronto, Ontario, Canada.

Douglas is a Past life regression Facilitator.

Certified in the science of complementary healing.

He now lives in the Tampa Bay area of Florida.